Carbon Tax: Deficit Reduction and Other Considerations

Jonathan L. Ramseur
Specialist in Environmental Policy

Jane A. Leggett
Specialist in Energy and Environmental Policy

Molly F. Sherlock
Specialist in Public Finance

September 17, 2012

Congressional Research Service
7-5700
www.crs.gov
R42731

CRS Report for Congress
Prepared for Members and Committees of Congress

Summary

The federal budget deficit has exceeded $1 trillion annually in each fiscal year since 2009, and deficits are projected to continue. Over time, unsustainable deficits can lead to reduced savings for investment, higher interest rates, and higher levels of inflation. Restoring fiscal balance would require spending reductions, revenue increases, or some combination of the two.

Policymakers have considered a number of options for raising additional federal revenues, including a carbon tax. A carbon tax could apply directly to carbon dioxide (CO_2) and other greenhouse gas (GHG) emissions, or to the inputs (e.g., fossil fuels) that lead to the emissions. Unlike a tax on the energy content of each fuel (e.g., Btu tax), a carbon tax would vary with a fuel's carbon content, as there is a direct correlation between a fuel's carbon content and its CO_2 emissions.

Carbon taxes have been proposed for many years by economists and some Members of Congress, including in the 112th Congress. If Congress were to establish a carbon tax, policymakers would face several implementation decisions, including the point and rate of taxation. Although the point of taxation does not necessarily reveal who bears the cost of the tax, this decision involves trade-offs, such as comprehensiveness versus administrative complexity.

Several economic approaches could inform the debate over the tax rate. Congress could set a tax rate designed to accrue a specific amount of revenues. Some would recommend setting the tax rate based on estimated benefits associated with avoiding climate change impacts. Alternatively, Congress could set a tax rate based on the carbon prices estimated to meet a specific GHG emissions target.

Carbon tax revenues would vary greatly depending on the design features of the tax, as well as market factors that are difficult to predict. One study estimated that a tax rate of $20 per metric ton of CO_2 would generate approximately $88 billion in 2012, rising to $144 billion by 2020. The impact such an amount would have on budget deficits depends on which budget deficit projection is used. For example, this estimated revenue source would reduce the 10-year budget deficit by 50%, using the 2012 baseline projection of the Congressional Budget Office (CBO). However, under CBO's alternative fiscal scenario, the same carbon tax would reduce the 10-year budget deficit by about 12%.

When deciding how to allocate revenues, policymakers would encounter key trade-offs: minimizing the costs of the carbon tax to "society" overall versus alleviating the costs borne by subgroups in the U.S. population or specific domestic industries. Economic studies indicate that using carbon tax revenues to offset reductions in existing taxes—labor, income, and investment—could yield the greatest benefit to the economy overall. However, the approaches that yield the largest overall benefit often impose disproportionate costs on lower-income households.

In addition, carbon-intensive, trade-exposed industries may face a disproportionate impact within a unilateral carbon tax system. Policymakers could alleviate this burden through carbon tax revenue distribution or through a border adjustment mechanism. Both approaches may entail trade concerns.

Contents

Introduction 1
Design and Implementation 4
   Point of Taxation 4
   Rate of Taxation 8
   Carbon Tax Effects on Fossil Fuel Prices 9
Framework for Evaluation 13
   Adequacy—The Potential to Generate Revenues 14
   Economic Efficiency 18
      Many Taxes Have Distortionary Effects 18
      Taxes May Correct Market Failures 19
      An Economically Efficient Carbon Tax Rate 20
   Equity 20
      Vertical Equity 20
      Horizontal Equity 21
      Individual Equity 21
      Generational Equity 21
   Operability 22
      Administrative Ease 22
      Consistency with Federal and International Norms and Standards 22
      Potential Perverse Effects 23
      Transparency 23
   Political Feasibility 24
Contribution to Deficit Reduction 24
Alternative Uses for Carbon Tax Revenues 26
   Distribute Carbon Tax Revenues to Households 26
   Address Economy-Wide Costs 29
   Assist Carbon-Intensive, Trade-Exposed Industries 30
Concluding Observations 31

Figures

Figure 1. Illustration of Options for Points of Taxation within the Energy Production-to-
   Consumption Chain 5
Figure 2. FY2011 Federal Receipts by Source 16
Figure 3. Annual Carbon Tax Revenues *in the Electricity Sector* 17
Figure 4. CBO Estimated Revenues from a $20/mtCO$_2$ Carbon Tax Compared to Two
   CBO Budget Deficit Projections 25

Tables

Table 1. Selected Sources of U.S. GHG Emissions and Potential Applications of a Carbon
   Tax 6

Table 2. CO_2 Emissions Per Unit of Energy for Fossil Fuels 10
Table 3. Estimated Taxes Levied on Fossil Fuels and Motor Gasoline Based on Selected Carbon Tax Rates.. 11
Table 4. Estimated Revenues from a CBO CO_2 Emissions Pricing Model.................................... 15
Table 5. Distributional Effects of Carbon Tax with Different Applications of Carbon Tax Revenues.. 28

Appendixes

Appendix. Carbon Tax and Carbon Pricing Proposals in the 111th Congress 33

Contacts

Author Contact Information... 33

Introduction

The federal budget deficit has exceeded $1 trillion annually in each fiscal year since 2009. In August 2012, the Congressional Budget Office (CBO) estimated an FY2012 budget deficit of $1.1 trillion, or 7.3% of gross domestic product (GDP).[1] Under CBO's alternative fiscal scenario, which assumes continuation of many current policies, the deficit as a percentage of GDP will be above 5% and rising from 2021 onward. Budget deficits are projected to continue, as the current mix of federal fiscal policies is widely viewed as being unsustainable in the long term.[2] Over time, unsustainable deficits can have negative macroeconomic consequences, including reduced savings for investment, higher interest rates, and higher levels of inflation.[3] Restoring fiscal balance will require spending reductions, revenue increases, or some combination of the two.

Policymakers have considered a number of options for raising additional federal revenues (see the text box below). One potential option is a carbon tax. Several economists and policy analysts from across the political spectrum have expressed interest in a carbon tax mechanism in recent years.[4] As of the date of this report, Members have introduced two carbon tax bills in the 112th Congress.[5] Several carbon price systems were proposed in the 111th Congress—as identified in the **Appendix**—most frequently as an efficient means to stimulate greenhouse gas (GHG) emission reductions. In addition, some countries have levied carbon taxes (or something similar) for over 20 years.[6]

---

[1] Congressional Budget Office, *An Update to the Budget and Economic Outlook: Fiscal Years 2012 to 2022*, Washington, DC, August 2012, http://www.cbo.gov/publication/43539.

[2] For background on budget baselines, see CRS Report R42362, *The Federal Budget: Issues for FY2013 and Beyond*, by Mindy R. Levit and CRS Report R41778, *Reducing the Budget Deficit: Policy Issues*, by Marc Labonte.

[3] See CRS Report RL33657, *Running Deficits: Positives and Pitfalls*, by D. Andrew Austin.

[4] A sampling of recent news and academic articles includes Mark Golden and Mark Shwartz, "Stanford's George Shultz on Energy: It's Personal," Stanford University, July 12, 2012; Jon Greenberg, "Laffer Carbon Tax: A Carbon Tax With a Twist to Please GOP—Maybe," *New Hampshire News*, December 14, 2011; Robert Inglis, "Fixing Market Distortions: A Free-Market Solution for Energy and Climate," University of Chicago Booth School of Business, April 11, 2012; Gilbert Metcalf, "Designing a Carbon Tax to Reduce U.S. Greenhouse Gas Emissions" *Review of Environmental Economics and Policy 3*, no. 1, pp. 63-83, September 2008; Brad Plumer, "Romney's One Big Idea on Climate—and Why He's Unlikely to Pursue It," *The Washington Post*, March 8, 2012; Amy Wolf, "Economist Arthur Laffer Proposes Taxing Pollution Instead of Income," Vanderbilt University, February 20, 2012.

[5] See the Save Our Climate Act of 2011 (H.R. 3242) and the Managed Carbon Price Act of 2012 (H.R. 6338).

[6] For a review of carbon taxes levied in other countries, see Jenny Sumner, et al., *Carbon Taxes: A Review of Experiences and Policy Design Considerations*, National Renewable Energy Laboratory, NREL/TP-6A2-47312, December 2009.

> **Options for Raising Federal Revenues**
>
> Congress could utilize one or more policy options to raise federal revenue. One frequently discussed option is to "broaden the tax base" by reforming or eliminating certain tax preferences. Some proponents of tax-base broadening suggest that any revenues raised should be used to reduce marginal rates, such that tax reform is revenue neutral.[7] Accordingly, tax-base broadening may have limited potential to generate additional federal revenues.[8] A second option for raising additional revenues is to increase other existing taxes. For example, Social Security reform might include increased payroll taxes.[9] Another option would be an increase in the motor fuel excise tax (e.g., the gas tax).[10] In addition, a number of alternative revenue sources could be used for deficit reduction, many of which are not widely used at the federal level. As one example, the United State could consider a value-added tax (VAT).[11]
>
> For more information, see CRS Report R41641, *Reducing the Budget Deficit: Tax Policy Options*, by Molly F. Sherlock and Congressional Budget Office, *Reducing the Deficit: Spending and Revenue Options*, Washington, DC, March 2011.

Other policy considerations, including environmental concerns, may also lead to consideration of a carbon tax. GHG in the atmosphere trap radiation as heat, warming the Earth's surface and oceans. The key human-related GHG is carbon dioxide (CO_2), primarily generated through the combustion of fossil fuels: coal, oil, and natural gas.[12] Although fossil fuels have facilitated economic growth in the United States and around the world, fossil fuel combustion has inadvertently raised the atmospheric concentration of CO_2 by about 40% over the past 150 years.[13] Almost all climate scientists agree[14] that these CO_2 increases have contributed to a warmer climate today, and that, if they continue, will contribute to future climate change.

---

[7] See, e.g., House Committee on the Budget Chairman Paul Ryan's "Path to Prosperity" report, released to accompany the FY2012 Budget Resolution (H.Con.Res. 34), which suggests eliminating unspecified tax expenditures to allow for reduced marginal tax rates. This report also states that eliminating tax expenditures would not be for the purpose of generating additional tax revenues. President Obama also expressed support for a revenue-neutral corporate tax reform as part of his 2012 State of the Union Address. Text of this address is available online at http://www.whitehouse.gov/the-press-office/2012/01/24/remarks-president-state-union-address.

[8] CRS Report R42435, *The Challenge of Individual Income Tax Reform: An Economic Analysis of Tax Base Broadening*, by Jane G. Gravelle and Thomas L. Hungerford.

[9] Both the Fiscal Commission and Debt Reduction Task Force plans would increase the wage base upon which payroll taxes are applied, thus increasing payroll tax revenues.

[10] The Fiscal Commission's deficit reduction proposal included a $0.15 per gallon increase in the federal motor fuel excise tax.

[11] See CRS Report R41602, *Should the United States Levy a Value-Added Tax for Deficit Reduction?*, by James M. Bickley and CRS Report R41708, *Value-Added Tax (VAT) as a Revenue Option: A Primer*, by James M. Bickley.

[12] Carbon dioxide (CO_2) accounted for approximately 84% of U.S. GHG emissions in 2010. Approximately 94% of the CO_2 emissions resulted from fossil fuel combustion activities. See U.S. Environmental Protection Agency, *Inventory of U.S. Greenhouse Gas Emissions and Sinks*, 1990-2010, April 2012, at http://epa.gov/climatechange/ghgemissions/usinventoryreport.html.

[13] For more information on climate change science, see CRS Report RL34266, *Climate Change: Science Highlights*, or CRS Report RL33849, *Climate Change: Science and Policy Implications*, both by Jane A. Leggett.

[14] See, for example, in 2007, the InterAcademy Council and the International Council of Academies of Engineering and Technological Sciences—both representing academies of sciences from dozens of nations—issued statements concurring that warming of the climate over the past 50 years is likely to have been caused by increased concentrations of GHG emissions in the atmosphere, with that increase having been caused by human-related GHG emissions. The views of a relatively small circle of scientists have been widely publicized as opposing mainstream conclusions; however, for these individuals the disagreement lies not in whether GHG increases have been caused by human activities, but whether these exert a "dangerous" influence on climate. See, for example, Robert M. Carter, "Knock, Knock: Where Is the Evidence for Dangerous Human-Caused Global Warming?" *Economic Analysis & Policy*, September 2008; S. Fred Singer, "Human Contribution to Climate Change Remains Questionable." *EOS Transactions* 80, April 20, 1999, pp. 183–187.

Many economists have argued that current fossil fuel prices reflect a *market failure,* because GHG emissions from fossil fuels contribute to current and future climate change, yet fossil fuel prices do not reflect climate change-related costs. Market failures distort economic efficiency by affecting consumer behavior. For example, energy consumers may make choices that are not in society's best interest, consuming more than the optimal amount of GHG emitting fuels, if prices do not reflect climate change-related costs.

Carbon taxes, or GHG fees, have been proposed as one means to correct such a market failure. Another option is a cap-and-trade program, which would attach a price to GHG emissions by limiting their generation.[15] To some extent, a carbon tax and cap-and-trade program would produce similar effects: Both would place a price on carbon, and both are estimated to increase the price of fossil fuels. Preference between the two approaches ultimately depends on which variable one prefers to control—GHG emissions or costs.[16]

A tax based on carbon content of fuels is different from a tax based on energy content, such as a Btu tax (see the text box below). Placing an emissions fee on CO_2 (and possibly other GHG emissions) could stimulate lower emissions and spur innovation in new lower-emitting technologies. A tax or fee based approach would allow markets to determine the level of investment in lower-emissions technologies. In addition, carbon tax revenues could be used to support multiple objectives, such as deficit reduction, or to replace existing taxes (e.g., payroll, income).

The 1993 Btu Tax

The deficit reduction package proposed by President Clinton in 1993 would have levied a tax based on energy content, measured in British thermal units (Btu). The 1993 Btu tax proposal called for a levy of 25.7 cents per million Btu, with a surcharge of 34 cents/million Btu on petroleum. The goals of the 1993 Btu tax proposal were to promote energy conservation and raise revenue. At the time, the proposed tax would have generated a new revenue stream of about $30 billion per year. The proposal was met with strong opposition and was not enacted; Congress ultimately enacted an (approximately 5-cent per gallon) increase in the motor fuels taxes.

The first section of this report examines carbon tax design and implementation issues, including the point of taxation, the rate of taxation, and the distribution of tax revenue. The second section discusses several carbon tax policy considerations: revenue potential, economic efficiency, equity, and operability. The final section highlights key issues related to the use of carbon tax revenues. Specifically, how might addressing the regressivity of a carbon tax diminish its revenue-raising potential, and what is the potential for a carbon tax to contribute to deficit reduction goals?

---

[15] Regulatory approaches can also be used to address market failures. Regulation-based emissions controls that reduce emissions would also be expected to increase the price of fossil fuels. The higher price faced by consumers may be closer to the true cost associated with consumption of emissions-producing fossil fuels.

[16] For a discussion see CRS Report R40242, *Carbon Tax and Greenhouse Gas Control: Options and Considerations for Congress*, by Jonathan L. Ramseur.

Design and Implementation

When establishing a carbon tax, there are several implementation decisions to be considered. Key considerations include (1) the point of taxation—where to impose the tax and what to tax; and (2) the rate of taxation. Information on how a carbon tax might affect fossil fuel prices is also provided.

Point of Taxation

The point of taxation would influence which entities would be required to (1) make tax payments based on emissions or emission inputs (e.g., fossil fuels), (2) monitor emissions or emission inputs, and (3) maintain records of relevant activities and transactions. The point of taxation does not necessarily reveal who bears the cost of the tax, as the cost may be passed on to intermediate producers or consumers. (This will be discussed in a later section.)

GHG emissions are generated throughout the economy by millions of discrete sources: smokestacks, vehicle exhaust pipes, households, commercial buildings, livestock, etc. Although CO_2 is the primary GHG at many sources, some sources predominantly emit non-CO_2 GHGs, such as methane.[17] When determining which sources and which GHG gases to control through a tax, policymakers would need to balance the benefits of comprehensiveness with administrative complexity and costs. Applying a carbon tax at the points of emissions from all GHG sources would present enormous logistical challenges.

CO_2 emissions are fairly easily to verify from large stationary sources, such as power plants. For almost 20 years, measurement devices have been installed in smokestacks of large facilities, reporting electronic information to the U.S. Environmental Protection Agency. For smaller sources, CO_2 emissions are a straightforward and accurate calculation based on the carbon content of fossil fuels consumed. Other GHG emissions, such as methane, nitrous oxides, sulfur hexafluoride, and others, could be more difficult or less reliable to verify. Thus, administrative costs and non-compliance risks would likely increase with a broader scope of an emissions tax. However, limiting the tax scope could result in perverse effects, with sources potentially shifting processes, facility size, or location to avoid taxes.

Policymakers may consider limiting the tax to sectors or sources that emit large percentages of the total U.S. GHG emissions or those that are relatively easy to measure. Or, the tax could be applied to reliable proxies for emissions in the production-to-emission chain. For example, the fossil fuel supply chain offers some options. As illustrated in **Figure 1**, potential emissions could be taxed at an "upstream" stage in that process, when the carbon-containing fossil fuel is first sold following production. Or, the point of taxation could, theoretically, be "downstream" where the pollution is released to the atmosphere.[18]

---

[17] Carbon tax proposals that apply only to CO_2 generally attach a price to a metric ton of CO_2 emissions (tCO_2). Non-CO_2 GHG emissions could be addressed by attaching a price to a metric ton of CO_2 emissions-equivalent (tCO_2e). This term of measure is used because GHGs vary by global warming potential (GWP). GWP is an index of how much a GHG may contribute to global warming over a period of time, typically 100 years. GWPs are used to compare gases to CO_2, which has a GWP of 1. For example, methane's GWP is 25, and thus a ton of methane is 25 times more potent a GHG than a ton of CO_2.

[18] A non-carbon example could be taxing nitrogen-based fertilizers based on their propensity to be emitted from (continued...)

Table 1 lists the top emission sources of six principal GHGs in the United States. These sources combine to account for approximately 95% of these gases (based on 2010 data).[19] **Table 1** also provides potential points of taxation that would cover the emissions from these sources. For example, policymakers could address CO_2 emissions from fossil fuel combustion and non-energy uses by levying an "upstream"[20] carbon tax on fewer than 2,300 entities—in aggregate 80% of U.S. GHG emissions.

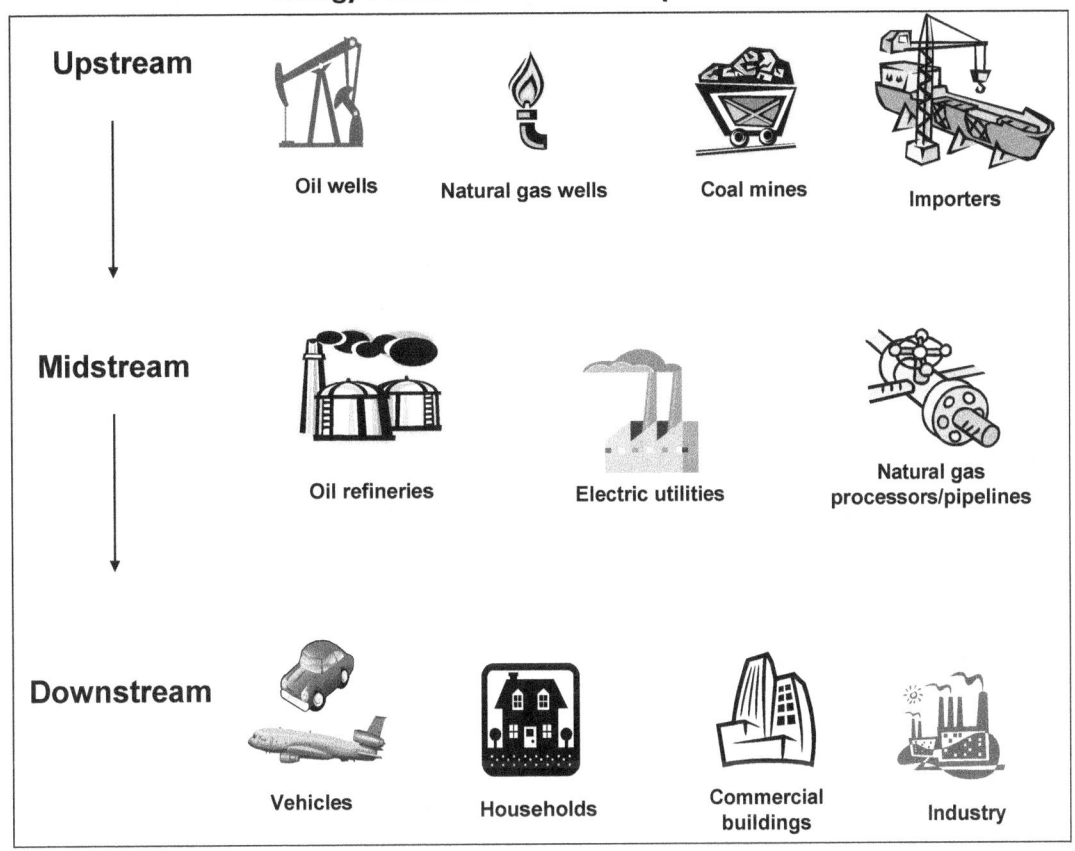

Figure 1. Illustration of Options for Points of Taxation within the Energy Production-to-Consumption Chain

Source: Prepared by CRS.

Note: Electric utilities could be listed as either downstream entities—because they are direct sources of emissions—or midstream, because their emissions are tied to the electricity consumption of their customers, the further downstream consumers.

(...continued)
agricultural soils as nitrous oxide (N_2O), another GHG the emissions of which would be difficult to measure directly.

[19] There are additional GHGs, but they are smaller influences (though rapidly growing in some cases) and less measured. Also, this does not account for the emissions and removals of carbon dioxide from the atmosphere by land use, land use change, and forestry (LULUCF). For more information, see CRS Report RL34266, *Climate Change: Science Highlights*, by Jane A. Leggett.

[20] An upstream approach would apply a carbon tax to fossil fuels when they enter the U.S. economy, either at the mine, wellhead, or another practical "chokepoint" in the production chain, such as oil refineries.

Alternatively, policymakers could employ a "downstream" approach, applying a carbon tax at the point where the gas is released to the atmosphere. For example, the FY2008 Consolidated Appropriations Act (P.L. 110-161) requires all large sources to annually *report* their GHG emissions to the EPA's Greenhouse Gas Reporting Program (GHGRP).[21] The program covers between 85-90% of all U.S. GHG emissions from approximately 13,000 facilities.[22]

Table 1. Selected Sources of U.S. GHG Emissions and Potential Applications of a Carbon Tax

GHG Emission Source	Percentage of U.S. GHG Emissions (2010 data)	Potential Carbon Tax Applications	
		Entity	Number
CO_2 from fossil fuel combustion:	78.9	Coal mines[a]	1,257
- electricity generation		or	
- transportation		Coal-fired power plants[b]	641
- industrial		Power plants[c] using imported coal[d]	26
- commercial/residential		Petroleum refineries[e]	150
		Petroleum importers[f]	220
		Natural gas processors[g]	530
		Natural gas importers[h]	45
N_2O from agricultural soils	3.0	Farms[i]	>2 million
CO_2 from non-energy use of fuels	1.8	Covered by the tax applied to fuels (above)[j]	
CH_4 from livestock (enteric fermentation)	2.1	Cattle operations[k]	967,440
CH_4 from landfills	1.6	Landfills[l]	1,800
HFCs from the substitution of ozone depleting substances	1.7	HFC manufacturers[m]	5
CH_4 from natural gas systems	3.1	Natural gas processors	530
CH_4 from coal mines	1.1	Coal mines[n]	1,257
CO_2 from iron/steel production	0.8	Raw steel production facilities;	116
		Integrated steel mills[o]	18
CO_2 from cement manufacturing	0.5	Cement plants[p]	118
CH_4 from manure management	0.8	Cattle operations;	967,440
		Swine operations[q]	65,640
Percentage of Total GHG Emissions	95.4		

Source: Prepared by CRS; GHG emission data from EPA, EPA, *Inventory of U.S. Greenhouse Gas Emissions and Sinks: 1990-2010*, April 2012; data for number of entities from multiple sources, cited in notes below.

---

[21] See 40 CFR Part 98.

[22] EPA, Fact Sheet: Mandatory Reporting of Greenhouse Gases (40 CFR Part 98), June 2011.

a. This figure accounts for mines in operation in 2010. EIA, *Coal Production and Number of Mines by State and Mine Type*, (2011).
b. In 2006, there were 641 plants with at least one coal-fired generating unit (EIA, 860 Database).
c. Number of plants comes from EIA database, Monthly Nonutility Fuel Receipts and Fuel Quality Data (Database 423). CRS was unable to determine the number of companies that act as coal importers, analogous to petroleum importers.
d. In 2006, the United States imported approximately 36 million short tons of coal (EIA, *Quarterly Coal Report* (2008), table 4)—3.5% of the amount of coal consumed domestically in that year (EIA, *Annual Coal Report 2006* (2007), table 26). Coal imports have increased by more than 200% since 2002.
e. This figure represents the number of "operable" refineries. EIA, *Refinery Capacity Report* (2008).
f. EIA, Company Level Imports (as of November 2008). Note that some of these companies may import only crude oil, whose emissions would be covered by the tax at the domestic refineries. Thus, this figure represents an upper bound of petroleum product importers potentially subject to a carbon tax.
g. EIA, Natural Gas Processing: The Crucial Link Between Natural Gas Production and Its Transportation to Market (2006).
h. This includes pipelines and liquefied natural gas facilities. EIA, *About U.S. Natural Gas Pipelines* (as of September 2008).
i. U.S. Department of Agriculture, *Farms, Land in Farms, and Livestock Operations: 2007 Summary* (2008). The resource defines a farm as "any place from which $1,000 or more of agricultural products were produced and sold, or normally would have been sold, during the year."
j. Fossil fuels are used for a wide range of non-energy purposes. EPA estimates that of the total carbon consumed for non-energy purposes, approximately 62% is stored in products, and not released to the atmosphere (EPA, *Inventory of U.S. Greenhouse Gas Emissions and Sinks: 1990-2006* (April 2008), tables 3-14 and 3-15). The 2% value in Table 4 represents the emissions. In an upstream carbon tax system, fuels would be taxed before they are used. Congress could choose to consider providing tax credits for the amount of carbon stored in products.
k. U.S. Department of Agriculture, *Farms, Land in Farms, and Livestock Operations: 2007 Summary* (2008).
l. EPA, Inventory of U.S. Greenhouse Gas Emissions and Sinks: 1990-2006 (April 2008), citing BioCycle, 15th Annual BioCycle Nationwide Survey: The State of Garbage in America (2006).
m. Intergovernmental Panel on Climate Change, Safeguarding the Ozone Layer and the Global Climate System, Issues related to Hydrofluorocarbons and Perfluorocarbons (2005), Figure 11.1.
n. Methane from underground mines, which accounts for about 61% of coal mine methane, is removed through ventilation systems for safety reasons. These emissions would be easier to monitor under a carbon tax than aboveground coal mine methane emissions.
o. Data from U.S. Geological Survey, Mineral Commodity Summary, Iron and Steel Production (2008), at http://minerals.usgs.gov/minerals/pubs/commodity/iron_&_steel/.
p. Cement manufacturing information from Portland Cement Association, at http://www.cement.org/basics/cementindustry.asp.
q. U.S. Department of Agriculture, *Farms, Land in Farms, and Livestock Operations: 2007 Summary* (2008). Other animals—chickens, horses, and sheep—contribute approximately 10% of the total emissions from manure (EPA, *Inventory of U.S. Greenhouse Gas Emissions and Sinks: 1990-2006* (April 2008), table 6-6).

Rate of Taxation

Although setting the carbon tax rate would likely involve political considerations, several economic approaches could be used to inform the debate. As a public finance instrument, the tax rate could be based on the estimated revenues needed to reduce or eliminate projected budget deficits.[23] This approach would be challenging, because estimates of future budget deficits (and thus the revenues needed to address them) are "inherently uncertain."[24] Moreover, a carbon tax would have some impact on the overall economy (and thus the overall tax base) that would make such a calculation more difficult.

Alternatively, the tax rate could be tied to climate change objectives. For example, Congress could set a tax rate based on the estimated benefits associated with avoiding climate change impacts. Some economists would say that the optimal level of a carbon tax would be at the "marginal cost of climate change," which is the incremental cost of damages of one more ton of emissions. This is sometimes called the Social Cost of Carbon (SCC).[25] The rate could include, as well, the cost of incremental damages of ocean acidification and other possible effects associated with carbon emissions (e.g., related air pollution).[26]

Estimates of the risks of GHG emissions are uncertain and cover a wide range. Analysts must place monetary values on goods and services that may be difficult or controversial to estimate, such as human health/life, water supplies, agricultural production, recreational activities. In addition, the element of time particularly complicates the valuation. The factor of time would demand a consideration of what global society should be willing to pay *now* to avoid *future* damages due to additional emissions generated *today*.[27] In short, basing the tax rate on a precise estimate of GHG emission-related risks would present extraordinary challenges.[28]

---

[23] The ability of a carbon tax to contribute to deficit reduction is analyzed in greater detail elsewhere in this report. See the section "Contribution to Deficit Reduction" below.

[24] Congressional Budget Office, *The 2012 Long-Term Budget Outlook*, June 2012.

[25] The SCC has been estimated for the purposes of allowing government agencies to consider social benefits from reduced carbon emissions in cost-benefit analysis. Details on the SCC for this purpose can be found in Interagency Working Group on the Social Cost of Carbon, United States Government, *Technical Support Document: Social Cost of Carbon for Regulatory Impact Analysis Under Executive Order 12866*, February 2010. SCC estimates are also provided in William D. Nordhaus, *Estimates of the Social Cost of Carbon: Background and Results from the Rice-2011 Model*, National Bureau of Economic Research, Working Paper 17540, Cambridge, MA, October 2011.

[26] These costs may be estimated simultaneously, or separately, as is done in National Academy of Sciences, *Hidden Costs of Energy: Unpriced Consequences of Energy Production and Use*, 2010; and Michael Greenstone and Adam Looney, *A Strategy for America's Energy Future: Illuminating Energy's Full Costs*, The Hamilton Project, Strategy Paper, May 2011.

[27] A critical and controversial assumption here is the discount rate used to discount future dollars into a present value. The use of low discount rates, such as some analyzed in Nicholas Stern's 2007 *Review on the Economics of Climate Change*, imply that aggressive policy action should be taken today to address future costs associated with climate change. Higher discount rates, such as those favored by William Nordhaus, would recommend applying fewer of today's resources to addressing climate change in the future (see William D. Nordhaus, "A Review of the Stern Review on the Economics of Climate Change," *Journal of Economic Literature*, vol. 45, no. 3 (September 2007), pp. 686-702.) Higher discount rates mean that costs in the future are worth less today, and less investment is warranted in the present to address future costs of climate change impacts. On the other hand, a fairness issues is raised by some in that high discount rates place little value on costs borne by generations yet to be born, whose preferences are generally not reflected in current generations' discount rates. There is little agreement in the economics community on appropriate discount rates to value such inter-generational problems.

[28] For further details see CRS Report R40242, *Carbon Tax and Greenhouse Gas Control: Options and Considerations for Congress*, by Jonathan L. Ramseur. See also the section on economics-based policy approaches in CRS Report (continued...)

An alternative climate change approach would involve basing the tax rate on an estimate of the carbon price needed to meet a specific GHG emissions target. Such estimates, though relatively more certain than the SCC, are similarly based on multiple assumptions. Accordingly, estimates of carbon prices in hypothetical carbon reduction schemes have varied dramatically. For example, multiple parties prepared such estimates during the development of H.R. 2454 (in the 111th Congress), which intended to reduce GHG emissions to 17% below their 2005 levels by 2020.[29] The emission allowance price estimates ranged from $16/metric tons of CO_2 equivalent ($mtCO_2e$) to $49/$tCO_2e$ in 2015, with the estimated range increasing over time.[30] Moreover, it could be challenging to reach political agreement on the GHG emissions target sought as well as the tax rate that would achieve it.

Given the uncertainty in the above estimates and a desire to avoid "shocking" the economy with a sudden change in tax policy, some have proposed starting a carbon tax with a rate that is initially set at a low rate, with that rate rising annually as announced for a fixed period or indefinitely. This approach would have several potential advantages: it is simple to explain and understand; it provides predictability to investors and consumers; and it allows policymakers to hedge[31] against the risks of carbon emissions.

Carbon Tax Effects on Fossil Fuel Prices

Different fossil fuels generate different amounts of CO_2 emissions per unit of energy. Therefore, a carbon tax, which is based on CO_2 emissions, would levy a higher charge (per unit of energy) on some fuels than others. As indicated in **Table 2**, coal generates approximately 80% more CO_2 emissions per unit of energy than natural gas, and approximately 28% more emissions per energy than crude oil. These differences in emissions intensity would lead to different tax rates per unit of energy across different fuels in a carbon tax regime.

(...continued)

R41973, *Climate Change: Conceptual Approaches and Policy Tools*, by Jane A. Leggett.

[29] H.R. 2454 (the American Clean Energy and Security Act of 2009, often called the "Waxman-Markey" bill) passed the House on June 26, 2009.

[30] For more information, see CRS Report R40809, *Climate Change: Costs and Benefits of the Cap-and-Trade Provisions of H.R. 2454*, by Larry Parker and Brent D. Yacobucci.

[31] To "hedge" is to insure oneself against losses. Investors typically face uncertainty and may use "hedging" as a strategy to reduce losses if/when adverse conditions occur. Investors may take actions that would offset the risk of another investment. Many analysts have recommended that policymakers hedge against future climate change risks by making investments, perhaps at a lower rate of return than other options, that would make sense whether or not future climate change is seriously adverse. For example, investing in low-emitting technologies may be one kind of hedge against climate change; stimulating such investments through a carbon tax may also be considered a hedge by many.

Table 2. CO_2 Emissions Per Unit of Energy for Fossil Fuels

Fossil Fuel	CO_2 Emissions Per Unit of Energy (million metric tons/quadrillion BTU)
Coal	96
Crude oil	75
Natural gas	53

Source: Prepared by CRS, based on Energy Information Administration (EIA), "Emissions Factors and Global Warming Potentials," updated January 2011, at http://www.eia.gov/oiaf/1605/emission_factors.html.

Notes: Coal emissions intensity values vary by type of coal, from 93-104 million metric tons/quadrillion BTU. The value above is for coal use in the electric power sector. The natural gas value above is the weighted national average of all uses, as prepared by EIA.

Table 3 includes estimates of the tax levied on fossil fuels and motor gasoline at different carbon tax rates. The change in price that consumers would see would likely not be the same as the carbon tax. Carbon taxes could affect fuel prices in complex ways. For example, energy consumers, to the extent possible, would likely shift their preferences to less expensive fuels, and the underlying prices of the fuels would change. Actual price increases that result from the illustrative carbon taxes in **Table 3** would depend on whether

- a carbon tax is applied at the beginning of the production process ("upstream") to fossil fuels (**Figure 1**);
- the price impacts are passed through to end-users and not absorbed by upstream energy producers or midstream entities (such as retailers); and
- consumers modify their behavior in the marketplace—energy conservation, fuel substitution, etc.

Table 3. Estimated Taxes Levied on Fossil Fuels and Motor Gasoline Based on Selected Carbon Tax Rates

Carbon Tax Rate[a]	Coal	Crude Oil	Natural Gas	Motor Gasoline
$5/mtCO$_2$	$9.50/short ton	$2.15/barrel	$0.25/mcf[b]	$0.05/gallon
$15/mtCO$_2$	$28.50/short ton	$6.45/barrel	$0.75/mcf	$0.15/gallon
$25/mtCO$_2$	$47.50/short ton	$10.75/barrel	$1.25/mcf	$0.25/gallon
$50/mtCO$_2$	$95.00/short ton	$21.50/barrel	$2.50/mcf	$0.50/gallon

CO$_2$ Emissions Intensities Used in Above Comparison

	Coal	Crude Oil	Natural Gas	Motor Gasoline
Metric tons of CO$_2$ (mtCO$_2$) per unit of fuel	1.9 mtCO$_2$/short ton[c]	0.43 mtCO$_2$/barrel[d]	0.05 mtCO$_2$/mcf[e]	0.01 mtCO$_2$/gallon[f]

Recent Market Prices for Each Fuel Type: Average Price Between 2000-2010 (2005 dollars)

Coal Type ($/short ton)[g]	Production Location ($/barrel)	Economic Sector ($/mcf)	Unleaded Regular ($/gallon): $2.14
Bituminous coal: $37	Domestic first purchase price:[h] $47	Residential: $11	
Sub-bituminous: $9	Import landed costs:[i] $48	Commercial: $10	
Lignite: $14		Industrial: $6	
Anthracite: $48		Transportation: $8	
		Electric power: $6	

Source: Prepared by CRS. CRS calculated the estimated taxes for each fuel by multiplying a carbon tax rate by the CO$_2$ emissions intensities for each fuel. CRS generated these inputs (the last row of the table) from the CO$_2$ coefficients (i.e., CO$_2$ emissions per quadrillion BTU) and thermal conversion factors (i.e., BTU per fuel unit) for each fuel. CO$_2$ coefficients are from EIA, "Emissions Factors and Global Warming Potentials," updated January 2011, at http://www.eia.gov/oiaf/1605/emission_factors.html; thermal conversion factors from EIA, *Annual Energy Review 2010*, October 2011, Appendices A1 (motor gasoline), A2 (crude oil), A4 (natural gas), and A5 (coal).

Fuel prices: Coal prices from EIA, *Annual Energy Review 2010*, Table 7.9, October 2011. Crude oil prices from Table 5.18 (domestic) and Table 5.19 (imported). CRS converted the nominal dollar values in Table 5.19 to $2005, using the GDP implicit price deflator provided in Appendix D of the *Annual Energy Review 2010*. Natural gas prices from Table 6.8. Gasoline prices from Table 5.24.

a. The tax rates in the table were selected for comparison purposes. The initial carbon tax rates in recent legislative proposals fall within the range identified above. Most proposals include annual rate increases, some of which generating tax rates that would approach the upper end of the range after several years.

b. MCF is thousand cubic feet.

c. This value represents the CO_2 coefficient for coal (electric power sector) and the thermal conversion factor for coal consumption from the electric power sector (2010).

d. This value represents the CO_2 coefficient for crude oil and the thermal conversion factor for "unfinished oil."

e. This value represents CO_2 coefficient for natural gas ("weighted national average") and the thermal conversion factor for end-use sectors (2010).

f. This value represents the CO_2 coefficient for "motor gasoline" and the thermal conversion factor for motor gasoline (conventional).

g. Bituminous and Subbituminous coal, in aggregate, accounted for 93% of U.S. coal production in 2010 (EIA, *Annual Energy Review 2010*, Table 7.2, October 2011).

h. EIA defines this price as "the price for domestic crude oil reported by the company that owns the crude oil the first time it is removed from the lease boundary." (*Annual Energy Review 2010*, Glossary).

i. EIA defines this price as "Crude Oil Landed Cost: The price of crude oil at the port of discharge, including charges associated with purchasing, transporting, and insuring a cargo from the purchase point to the port of discharge. The cost does not include charges incurred at the discharge port (e.g., import tariffs or fees, wharfage charges, and demurrage)." (*Annual Energy Review 2010*, Glossary).

Framework for Evaluation

Policymakers may consider a carbon tax based on a number of policy motivations and potential benefits, including

- increased federal revenues,
- reduced federal budget deficits,
- reduced GHG emissions, climate change, and ocean acidification,[32]
- enhanced energy security,
- improved economic efficiency, and/or
- reduced tax rates from other revenue sources.

In recent years in the United States, most carbon tax proposals have aimed primarily to discourage GHG emissions.[33] In these proposals, a tax or fee would be levied on GHG emissions or the inputs (i.e., fossil fuels) that lead to emissions. The tax or fee raises the price of the emission-generating products, and therefore can, on the one hand, motivate suppliers to reduce the emissions involved in making the product and, on the other hand, encourage consumers to buy less of the product. This policy instrument sets the tax (cost) per unit of emissions and relies on private decision-makers to find the most efficient means to reduce the emissions. A carbon tax is one of several "market mechanisms" that relies on the efficiencies of markets to maximize cost-effectiveness.

Though this policy instrument is commonly called a "carbon tax," its application could be broader than this term suggests. First, the policy may apply not just to CO_2 emissions, but also to multiple GHGs (e.g., methane or sulfur hexafluoride), including some that may have no molecular carbon.[34] Second, if the levy's primary purpose were to charge those who use the atmosphere to absorb the full cost of their GHG emissions, the levy might instead be considered a "user fee."[35] Regardless, this report uses the term "carbon tax," because this report focuses on the policy instrument's potential to raise revenues and reduce the federal budget deficit.

---

[32] For explanation of how carbon emissions may acidify oceans and the potential effects, see CRS Report R40143, *Ocean Acidification*, by Eugene H. Buck and Peter Folger.

[33] Most legislative attention to reduce GHG emissions, however, has been given to emissions cap-and-trade schemes and tax incentives. See for example, CRS Report R40242, *Carbon Tax and Greenhouse Gas Control: Options and Considerations for Congress*, by Jonathan L. Ramseur; CRS Report R40556, *Market-Based Greenhouse Gas Control: Selected Proposals in the 111th Congress*, by Brent D. Yacobucci, and Jonathan L. Ramseur. For other policy instruments, see CRS Report R41973, *Climate Change: Conceptual Approaches and Policy Tools*, by Jane A. Leggett, and CRS Report R41769, *Energy Tax Policy: Issues in the 112th Congress*, by Molly F. Sherlock and Margot L. Crandall-Hollick.

[34] Non-carbon GHGs could be subject to the tax based on their contribution to global warming in relation to CO_2. Global warming potential (GWP) is an index of how much a GHG may contribute to the average annual increase in worldwide temperature integrated over a period of time, typically 100 years but sometimes as short as 20 years. GWPs are used to compare gases to carbon dioxide, which has a GWP of 1. For example, methane's GWP is 25, and is thus 25 times more potent a GHG than CO_2. The GWPs listed in this report are from: Intergovernmental Panel on Climate Change, *Climate Change 2007: The Physical Science Basis,* 2007, p. 212.

[35] The Congressional Budget Office defines user charges as fees or taxes that are based on benefits individuals or firms receive from the federal government or that in some way compensate for costs they might impose on society or its (continued...)

There are a number of issues to be considered when evaluating tax policy proposals.[36] The following sections analyze a generic carbon tax option using the criteria listed below:

- *adequacy*—the ability to generate a desired amount of revenues;
- *economic efficiency*—the potential to enhance or diminish the productivity of the U.S. economy;
- *equity*—the subjective determination of a proposal's fairness;
- *operability*—the combination of multiple factors, including administrative ease, transparency, avoidance of perverse outcomes, and consistency with federal and international norms and standards;[37] and
- *political feasibility*—the likelihood of enactment given a tax's visibility to the public and public opinion, differential regional implications, contribution to deficit reduction or other objectives, pledges made by some lawmakers not to raise taxes, etc.[38]

Adequacy—The Potential to Generate Revenues

The revenues that would be generated under a carbon tax vary greatly depending on the design features of the tax, namely the tax scope (i.e., base) and rate, as well as such independent factors as prices in global energy markets. Several recent proposals to price or tax carbon, where revenue estimates are available, are presented below.

In 2011, the Congressional Budget Office (CBO) evaluated a hypothetical cap-and-trade program in which CO_2 emission allowances (i.e., permits to emit one metric ton of CO_2 emissions) would be sold at auction and traded in a carbon market. The auction revenues generated in this program would be analogous to tax revenues under a carbon tax system. CBO estimated the allowance price, which, under an actual program, would be determined by market forces, would begin at $20 per metric ton of CO_2 (mtCO_2) in 2012 and increase 5.6% annually. This allowance price estimate, and its projected annual increase, is akin to a prescribed carbon tax rate. CBO estimated that such a regime would raise $1.2 trillion over the 2012 to 2021 budget window (**Table 4**).

(...continued)

resources. See Congressional Budget Office, *The Growth of Federal User Charges*, August 1993. See also GAO, *Federal User Fees: A Design Guide*, GAO-08-386SP, May 2008.

[36] See, for example, the evaluation criteria identified in American Institute of CPAs. "AICPA Tax Policy and Tax Reform Materials: No.1 Guiding Principles of Good Tax Policy: A Framework for Evaluating Tax Proposals", 2001, available at http://www.aicpa.org/INTERESTAREAS/TAX/RESOURCES/TAXLEGISLATIONPOLICY/Pages/TaxReform.aspx.

[37] See this categorization in, for example, Joseph T. Sneed, "The Criteria of Federal Income Tax Policy," *Stanford Law Review* 17, no. 4 (April 1, 1965) pp. 567-613; B.G. Peters, *The Politics of Taxation: A Comparative* Perspective, 1991, at http://www.tau.ac.il/law/cegla3/tax2/9%20The%20Politics%20of%20Taxation%20-%20Peters.pdf.

[38] For example, the Taxpayer Protection Pledge promoted by the Americans for Tax Reform interest group; Information at http://www.atr.org/taxpayer-protection-pledge and http://www.atr.org/about-grover.

Table 4. Estimated Revenues from a CBO CO₂ Emissions Pricing Model
$20/mtCO$_2$ in 2012, increasing 5.6% annually (billions of dollars)

	2012	2013	2014	2015	2016	2017	2018	2019	2020	2021	2012-2016	2012-2021
Revenues	88	93	99	105	112	119	127	136	144	154	499	1,179

Source: Congressional Budget Office, *Reducing the Deficit: Spending and Revenue Options*, Washington, DC, March 2011, pp. 205-206.

Notes: The CBO assessment does not precisely describe the scope of its carbon tax scenario (i.e., which industries would be covered). Also, estimated revenues reflect reductions in income and payroll tax revenues that would result from the effects of a charge for emitting carbon.

As a point of reference for the above carbon tax revenue estimates, **Figure 2** identifies the major sources of federal receipts in FY2011. As the figure illustrates, the range of potential carbon tax revenues is comparable (at least in the early years of the carbon tax system) to the revenues collected from current federal excise taxes. Nearly half of all federal excise tax receipts come from taxes on gasoline and diesel fuels.[39]

Legislation introduced in the 112th Congress, the Save Our Climate Act of 2011 (H.R. 3242), would establish a carbon tax on domestic and imported fossil fuels, as well as the carbon content of biomass, municipal solid waste, and any organic material used as fuel. The tax rate would begin at $10 per short ton[40] of CO$_2$ emissions (tCO$_2$), increasing by $10 annually until total U.S. CO$_2$ emissions are 20% or less of CO$_2$ emissions in 1990. The bill states that it would reduce the federal budget deficit by a $480 billion over ten years.

Other revenue estimates have been made in recent years of carbon taxes considered or included in a number of deficit and debt reduction proposals.[41] As one example, in 2010, the bipartisan Debt Reduction Task Force (Domenici-Rivlin) considered, but did not ultimately recommend, a tax on CO$_2$ emissions. The report estimated that a tax of $23 per ton of CO$_2$ emissions starting in 2018, increasing 5.8% annually, would raise approximately $1.1 trillion in cumulative revenues through 2025.[42]

---

[39] For data on federal excise tax collections, see Internal Revenue Service (IRS), Statistics of Income (SOI) Historical Table 20, http://www.irs.gov/taxstats/article/0,,id=175900,00.html.

[40] In this proposal, a ton is a short ton, or 2,000 pounds. Most of the more recent proposals and models use metric tons (or tonnes), which are 2,240 pounds.

[41] The Committee for a Responsible Federal Budget's (CRFB) online comparison tool is a good starting point for comparing various debt and deficit reduction proposals. This tool is available at http://crfb.org/compare/.

[42] Bipartisan Policy Center, *Restoring America's Future: Reviving the Economy, Cutting Spending and Debt, and Creating a Simple, Pro-Growth Tax System*, November 2010, http://bipartisanpolicy.org/projects/debt-initiative/about.

Figure 2. FY2011 Federal Receipts by Source

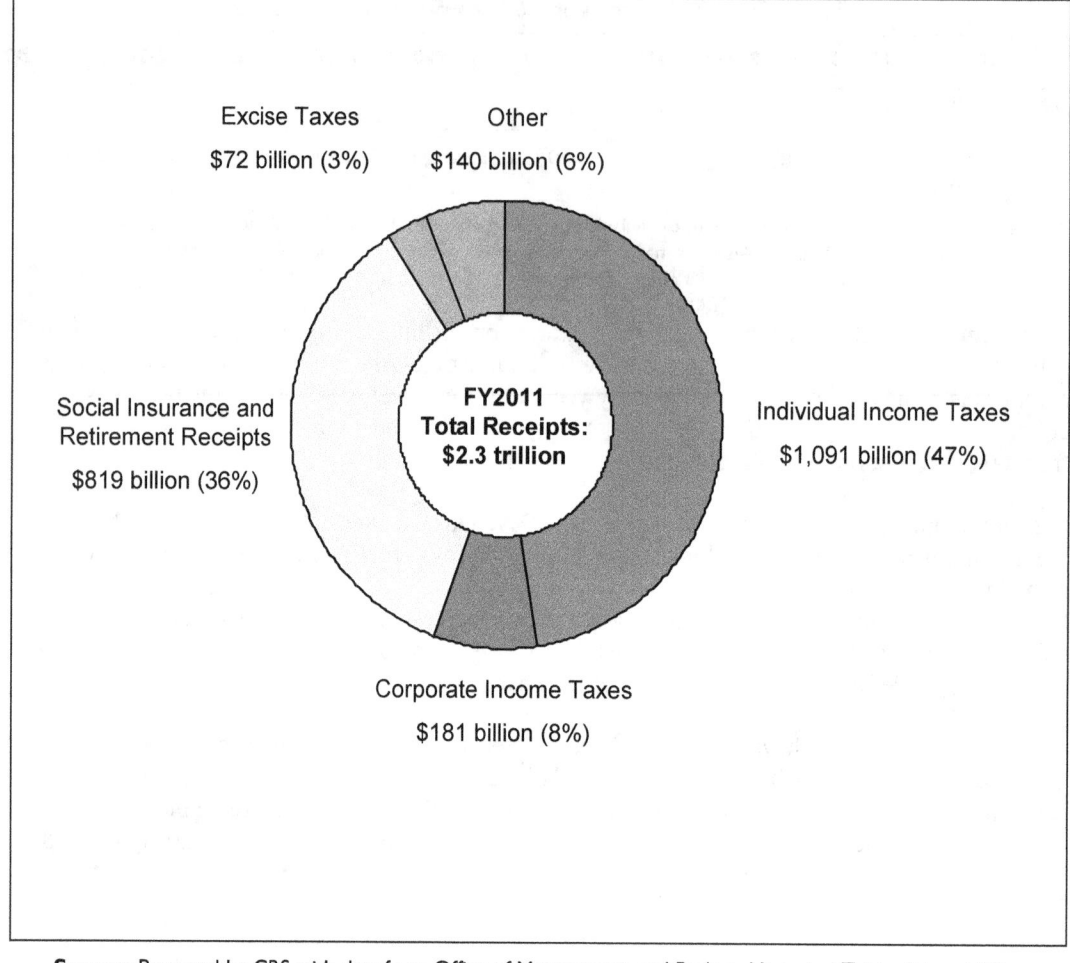

Source: Prepared by CRS with data from Office of Management and Budget, Historical Tables 2.1 and 2.2, at http://www.whitehouse.gov/omb/budget/historicals.

In addition to a carbon tax design, a 2012 Resources for the Future (RFF) study[43] identified several factors—electricity demand and natural gas prices—that could influence carbon tax revenue. The study found that the magnitude of these factors' influence increases as the tax rate increases. **Figure 3** illustrates the RFF study findings.

In **Figure 3**, RFF compares tax revenue estimates using assumptions from EIA's 2009 and 2011 *Annual Energy Outlook* (AEO) publications. According to the study, the AEO assumptions regarding future electricity demand and fuel prices, namely natural gas, varied dramatically between the 2009 and 2011 versions. These variances lead to different estimates of potential carbon tax revenue. For example, as illustrated in **Figure 3**, estimated revenues in 2020 from a tax rate of $25/mtCO$_2$ would vary across scenarios by about $10 billion. A $40/mtCO$_2$ tax rate would generate an estimated revenue range across scenarios of almost $20 billion in 2020.

---

[43] Karen Palmer et al., *The Variability of Potential Revenue from a Tax on Carbon*, Resources for the Future, May 2012.

Further, **Figure 3** highlights a key result of a carbon tax that may affect its ability to provide a reliable source of revenue. Note that the tax revenues *in the electricity sector* begin to decline around 2030 with the $40/mtCO$_2$ tax rate. The study concluded this decline is due to a diminishing reliance on fossil fuels and relatively greater reliance on low-carbon energy sources, such as renewables and nuclear.

The projected scenario in **Figure 3** highlights a fundamental revenue adequacy concern associated with a carbon tax approach: if a primary goal of a carbon tax is to reduce its own tax base (i.e., carbon emissions), would this tax provide a reliable stream of revenues over time? With revenue reliability as a primary goal, governments impose taxes on activities to which producers and consumers are not very price-sensitive. In other words, the imposed taxes lead to minimal changes in market behavior. Researchers debate how much producers and consumers would respond to a tax on GHG emissions by reducing emissions or switching to goods and services that generate fewer emissions (because they embody lower taxes). With a higher degree of responsiveness, either revenues would decline or the tax rate per ton of emissions would need to increase over time to maintain the revenue stream (assuming that maintaining certain revenue stream is determined to be a policy objective).

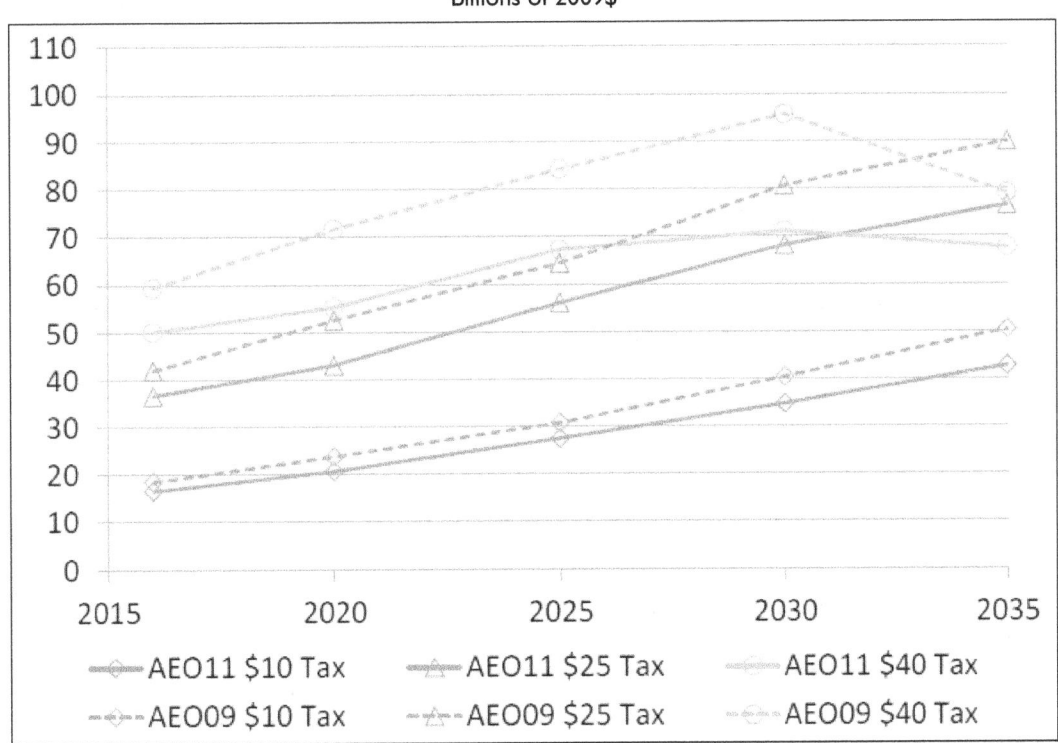

Figure 3. Annual Carbon Tax Revenues *in the Electricity Sector*
Billions of 2009$

Source: Karen Palmer et al, *The Variability of Potential Revenue from a Tax on Carbon*, Resources for the Future, May 2012.

Notes: AEO09 and AEO11 refer to EIA's 2009 and 2011 *Annual Energy Outlook*. The carbon taxes are levied on metric tons of CO2 emissions (mtCO$_2$), with rates starting in 2016 and growing 5% annually.

Economic Efficiency

Economic theory suggests that a carbon tax could improve the efficiency of the economy by at least three means:[44]

- First, markets could produce a more optimal mix of goods and services if the costs of emitting GHG while manufacturing products, providing services, or using goods were "internalized" into market prices; producers and consumers would more fully respond to the full costs of their decisions, resulting in a more economically efficient outcome;

- Second, a tax on an activity that yields pollutants, such as GHG emissions,[45] would discourage the polluting activity and therefore could be more efficient than an alternative tax that yields the same revenues but discourages a beneficial activity (e.g., investment); and

- Third, adding a smaller tax on a new activity, such as potential carbon emissions, could be less distortionary to production and consumption than increasing the tax rate on currently taxed activities.[46]

The difficulty associated with setting an optimal carbon tax rate makes achieving potential efficiency gains challenging. Further, a stand-alone carbon tax (e.g., one where revenues were not used to offset other taxes) could have efficiency costs, as a carbon tax would increase existing distortions on inputs in the production process. The difficulty of implementing an efficiency-enhancing carbon tax is compounded in a tax system that already contains a number of distortionary taxes.[47]

Many Taxes Have Distortionary Effects[48]

Many people are concerned about several potentially "distortionary" effects of taxes on society. Many economists consider that taxes take money away from people and change the relative prices of goods and services compared to what they would be without taxes; thus, taxes are considered "distortionary" by altering free market decisions. To minimize distortions (and generate a reliable stream of revenues), governments often prefer to tax products or activities for which consumer

---

[44] Achieving economic efficiency means using limited resources such that the production of goods and services is maximized at the lowest possible cost.

[45] Though some people contend that GHG emissions may not pose adverse risks, this is the view of a minority of scientific and economic experts in the field of climate change, and the suggestion of no adverse risk is not supported by empirical evidence to date.

[46] This assumes that a new tax on carbon would ultimately apply to a broader base, and not simply compound existing distortions to labor and capital that exist in the current tax system. A stand-alone carbon tax could compound existing tax-induced distortions in labor markets, for example. Thus, a carbon tax could have efficiency costs to the extent that a carbon tax further reduces labor supply.

[47] For an extensive theoretical exposition of conditions under which a carbon tax can enhance economic efficiency, see A. Lans Bovenberg and Lawrence H. Goulder, "Environmental Taxation and Regulation," in *Handbook of Public Economics*, ed. Alan J. Auerback and Martin Feldstein, vol. 3 (Elsevier, 2002), pp. 1471-1545.

[48] A head tax, or a lump-sum tax levied on individuals regardless of income or wealth, is considered a non-distortionary tax since individuals cannot avoid the tax by changing their behavior. Since most taxes can be avoided with changes in behavior, non-distortionary taxes often do not exist in practice.

demands are relatively insensitive to price increases.[49] Some of these taxed items are recognized as essential or socially desirable, such as income, employment, and investment. Taxes may also be "distortionary" because they discourage a taxed but beneficial activity. For example, many economists argue that payroll and income taxes are distortionary because they discourage employment and investment.[50] If these taxes were reduced, the incentives to hire/work and invest, they argue, would be greater.

Also, as tax rates (i.e., the tax per unit of a product or service) increase, they become *more* distortionary. That is, higher tax rates have greater potential to shift choices away from optimal "free market" outcomes. As an example, consumers may respond proportionately more strongly to a $1.00 tax per gallon on gasoline than a $0.20 tax per gallon (in other words, the efficiency losses associated with a tax increase exponentially with the tax rate). Thus, applying lower tax rates to broader tax bases can help minimize inefficiencies.[51]

Taxes May Correct Market Failures

Not all results from economic activity are considered desirable—pollution being one example. When producers or consumers discharge pollution—including GHG emissions—to another person's private property or a publicly shared resource—such as the atmosphere—without paying to do so, they are not paying for the full cost of a product or activity. Economists would describe this outcome as a "market failure," because the costs associated with GHG emissions are not captured in the economic decision process. Economists contend that levying a charge on GHG emission would be an economically efficient way to correct the failure.[52] For example, in terms of environmental policy, fossil fuel prices do not reflect the costs—related to climate change and ocean acidification damages—associated with the GHG emissions. A pollution discharge fee could internalize these external costs into market prices.

A primary argument in favor of a carbon tax is that it would, in theory, increase the efficiency of markets by discouraging "bad" activities. A carbon tax would discourage pollution that imposes costs on others who do not necessarily benefit from the polluting activity. These may include future generations that bear the dislocations of climate change, or fishery sectors in developing countries that experience lower yields in acidified oceans.

A carbon tax would encourage energy consumers—for example, power plants, industry, households, etc.—to (1) switch to less carbon-intensive fuels; (2) use less energy or use energy more efficiently; and (3) prefer products or services that are lower-priced by virtue of incorporating less emission tax. Each of these activities would reduce GHG emissions compared to a business-as-usual track and could improve economic efficiency.

---

[49] In economics parlance, a small response of consumer demand may be termed "price inelastic."

[50] See, e.g., Gilbert Metcalf, *A Green Employment Tax Swap: Using a Carbon Tax to Finance Payroll Tax Relief*, 2007; Nathaniel Keohane and Sheila Olmstead, *Markets and the Environment* (Island Press, 2007); Ian Parry "Fiscal Interactions and the Case for Carbon Taxes over Grandfathered Carbon Permits," in *Climate Change Policy*, Dieter Helm, editor, (Oxford University Press, 2005).

[51] A theoretical exposition illustrating how marginal distortionary effects rise with the rate of taxation can be found in Jonathan Gruber, *Public Finance and Public Policy* (New York: Worth Publishers, 2007), pp. 584-585.

[52] Imposing regulations can also correct for market failures.

An Economically Efficient Carbon Tax Rate[53]

To improve efficiency, a carbon tax would need to be set at the "right" level. According to basic economic theory, the "right" level would be one that equilibrates the tax rate to the incremental harm, now and in the future, that a ton of GHG emissions imposes. To find this tax rate precisely, one would need to know the marginal costs of climate change and ocean acidification.

However, estimating the effects and placing a monetary value on them is both controversial and reliable only over a wide range. Hence, no consensus is likely to emerge regarding a precisely "right" carbon tax rate.[54] An analytical or political estimate is feasible but may not be the most economically efficient outcome. Further, setting carbon tax rates based on revenue needs for deficit reduction, or some other purpose, would not necessarily result in setting a rate that is proportional to the incremental harm of GHG emissions.

Equity

The "equity" or "fairness" of taxes can be evaluated by looking at how different parties are affected. How the burden of a tax is ultimately divided between different parties is described as the economic incidence of the tax.[55] To evaluate the subjective concepts of "equity" and "fairness" in tax policy, economists often examine two different types of equity: vertical and horizontal. In addition, some economists consider individual and generational equity. A complete policy analysis might consider the potential trade-off between economic efficiency and equity.[56] These four elements of tax equity are discussed below.

Vertical Equity

The notion of vertical equity suggests that those with a greater ability to pay should contribute more. Without some of tax revenue redistribution, carbon taxes are generally considered to be "regressive," because lower-income households generally spend a higher percentage of their income on energy-related goods and services than do higher-income households.[57] The actual or perceived regressivity of carbon or fuel taxes can have a strong influence on the political feasibility of the instrument.[58] For example, the coalition of advocates for low-income people and opponents of energy taxes arguably contributed to the failure of President Clinton's 1993 "Btu Tax" proposal (see the text box above), which was introduced as part of a deficit reduction package.

---

[53] A related discussion appears in the "Rate of Taxation" section above.

[54] For more information on the challenges of estimating the environmental and health costs of GHG emissions, see CRS Report R41973, *Climate Change: Conceptual Approaches and Policy Tools*, by Jane A. Leggett.

[55] This is in contrast to the statutory incidence, where the statutory incidence falls on the person responsible for remitting the tax to the tax authorities.

[56] See CRS Report R41641, *Reducing the Budget Deficit: Tax Policy Options*, by Molly F. Sherlock.

[57] See CRS Report R40841, *Assisting Households with the Costs of a Cap-and-Trade Program: Options and Considerations for Congress*, by Jonathan L. Ramseur and Libby Perl.

[58] See Stephen Moore, "Federal Budget Issue: Do We Need an Energy Tax?" National Center for Policy Analysis, June 1993, at http://www.ncpa.org/pub/bg127?pg=4, as an example of expressed concerns.

Particular carbon tax design elements could reduce its regressivity. For example, carbon tax revenues could be used to reduce other taxes (e.g., income) or be redistributed to lower-income households through a variety of funding mechanisms (see the section "Alternative Uses for Carbon Tax Revenues" below).

Horizontal Equity

Horizontal equity examines whether potential tax-payers with similar characteristics would receive equivalent tax treatment. Questions of horizontal equity may arise if particular industries or economic sectors that predominately emit non-CO_2 GHG emissions (e.g., methane) were exempted from the carbon tax regime, while industries or sectors of comparable size were included based on their CO_2 emissions.[59]

Individual Equity

Some people consider taxes unfair when they involve government interference in private transactions, including freedom to use one's resources as one chooses. This is sometimes considered a violation of "individual equity."[60] To minimize infringement of individual equity, some would argue that taxes should be levied on, and commensurate with, the benefit an individual receives from the taxed activity, or "benefit taxation."[61] (Proponents contend that not to violate individual equity would require that the tax be voluntary.) Some might counter that a carbon tax is a kind of "benefit taxation," levied on the benefit the carbon source receives by being allowed to discharge the pollution to the atmosphere.

Generational Equity

Are the burdens of taxation and benefits from governmental spending fairly distributed across generations? This is a particular concern in the context of the federal deficit and GHG-induced climate change, both of which would likely shift costs from the current generation to subsequent generations. At first glance, a carbon tax could potentially support generational equity by helping to slow or reduce GHG-induced climate change and by potentially reducing the deficit (depending on the fate of tax revenues).

However, an assessment of generational equity is complex. Some may argue that a carbon pricing mechanism would reduce the wealth of the current generation, consequently reducing the productive capacities of future generations. Moreover, some may argue that, instead of a carbon price approach, increased investment in technology would yield greater benefits for future generations. Others may counter that increased investments today may result in increased

---

[59] During the debates of the 1993 Btu tax proposal, exemptions allowed to various interests may have contributed to a perception of its unfairness. For one view of the politics of the Btu tax debate and demise, see Dawn Erlandson, "The Btu Tax Experience: What Happened and Why It Happened," *Pace Environmental Law Review* 12, no. 1, 1994.

[60] C. Eugene Steuerle, "And Equal (Tax) Justice for All?" in *Tax Justice: The Ongoing Debate,* edited by Joseph J. Thorndike and Dennis J. Ventry (Urban Institute Press, 2002).

[61] Discussions of individual equity and benefit taxation arise mostly in discussions of public finance for education, Social Security, and other kinds of programs that offer an explicit benefit. See, for example, American Academy of Actuaries, "Social Security Reform: Changes to the Benefit Formula and Taxation of Benefits" at http://www.actuary.org/pdf/socialsecurity/benefit_05.pdf; or Kent E. Portney, "Individual Equity And School Finance: Implications For Taxation And State Aid." *Journal of Education Finance* 2, no. 2, 1976.

consumption, providing minimal benefits for future generations and foregoing the opportunity to address climate change impacts. Such an outcome would disproportionately burden future generations.

Operability

Some tax options may be elegant in terms of economic theory but, in practice, present considerable logistical challenges. This section identifies some of the key administrative issues that might arise when implementing a carbon tax.

Administrative Ease

In previous debates over carbon taxes, which largely focused on discouraging GHG emissions, many proponents asserted that carbon taxes would be administratively simple compared to the principal emissions control alternatives—notably, a cap-and-trade program[62] or emissions performance standards. As with other comparisons, the relative advantage of a carbon tax would depend on the designs of the instrument alternatives under scrutiny.

Any new kind of tax would require new administrative systems, but a carbon tax system could potentially take advantage of existing frameworks. A well-developed administrative structure for collecting taxes already exists in the United States. In addition, approximately 13,000 facilities report annual GHG emissions to EPA.[63] Therefore, EPA already collects carbon tax emissions data covering about 90% of all U.S. GHG emissions. However, a tax program would presumably be administered by the Department of the Treasury. Transferring data should not be technically difficult, but broader cooperation across agencies would likely be necessary to share respective expertise and to promote compliance.

Consistency with Federal and International Norms and Standards

Policymakers might consider the degree to which a carbon tax is consistent with other policies that support other objectives: pollution control, energy affordability, national security. Superficially, carbon taxes would seem to be consistent with other GHG emission control standards, but would conflict with incentives to make fossil fuels more affordable.

In terms of linking a U.S. GHG emission reduction scheme with international efforts, a carbon tax may be at a disadvantage, because the most prominent international activity, namely the European Union's Emission Trading Scheme,[64] currently involves a cap-and-trade approach.

---

[62] A cap-and-trade system is arguably is more administratively complex than a tax. However, both systems, if they apply to all GHG and all large sources of emissions, involve many components. Moreover, as policymakers include more flexible design elements—primarily to improve efficiency and control price volatility—a cap-and-trade program would increase in complexity. It would be more costly to administer; more open to exploitation (for example, by traders of derivative financial instruments); potentially less transparent; and harder for regulators to ensure compliance.

[63] EPA's Greenhouse Gas Reporting Program in 40 CFR Part 98.

[64] See CRS Report R42392, *Aviation and the European Union's Emission Trading Scheme*, by Jane A. Leggett, Bart Elias, and Daniel T. Shedd.

Potential Perverse Effects

Some carbon pricing policies may yield unexpected and unwelcome results. For carbon taxes, one such "perverse effect" would be the potential to increase the cost of business activity in the United States. Over time, this could result in reduced revenue from both the carbon tax and other taxes.[65] This consideration has led some other countries to exempt energy-intensive manufacturers in specific or strategic sectors from energy or carbon taxes.[66]

In addition, a carbon tax could lead to emissions "leakage," if businesses moved operations overseas to avoid the tax. This outcome would depend on a number of factors, however, including relative fuel mixes, efficiencies of power production and transportation, border taxes, etc.

Transparency

Tax policies that are transparent may be more likely viewed as fair, as taxes being paid are understood by those responsible for paying the tax. In recent years, many have grown more skeptical of complex financial structures.[67] Potential complexity and opaqueness of a cap-and-trade program was one factor that led some advocates of GHG control policies to prefer carbon taxes as a policy instrument.

While a carbon tax could be designed to be simple and transparent, Congress could also choose to establish a carbon tax framework that rivals the complexity of a cap-and-trade program. For instance, policymakers could provide subsidies or exemptions to the fossil fuel industry or certain consumers (e.g., agricultural users) or enact incentives for producing, processing, and exporting fossil fuels. In addition, policymakers could allow for tax credits for carbon sequestration projects, similar to carbon offsets in a cap-and-trade regime.[68] As with carbon offsets in a cap-and-trade program, this would require a further level of administrative responsibilities, and potentially weaken the program.[69]

Ironically, transparency, particularly in regards to costs, could be a political liability for a carbon tax. Although both a carbon tax and a cap-and-trade program would impose higher energy costs, the costs from a cap-and-trade program would be more difficult to estimate, because the market would determine the price of emission allowances (and thus the overall costs of the program).

---

[65] The CBO takes this into account when estimating net revenues from a carbon tax.

[66] See CRS Report R40936, *An Overview of Greenhouse Gas (GHG) Control Policies in Various Countries*, by Jane A. Leggett et al.

[67] See CRS Report RL34488, *Regulating a Carbon Market: Issues Raised By the European Carbon and U.S. Sulfur Dioxide Allowance Markets*, by Mark Jickling and Larry Parker.

[68] The tax code already contains provisions allowing tax credits for carbon sequestration (see Internal Revenue Code §45Q).

[69] See CRS Report RL34436, *The Role of Offsets in a Greenhouse Gas Emissions Cap-and-Trade Program: Potential Benefits and Concerns*, by Jonathan L. Ramseur.

Political Feasibility

Certain stakeholders are likely to exercise strong opposition to a carbon tax. These include energy-intensive manufacturers, farmers, and regional energy interests—especially those whose asset values may fall with expected impacts on profitability of owned or leased coal and oil resources. One may look to numerous reviews of the histories of both the Clinton Btu tax proposal and more recent cap-and-trade bills for lengthier views regarding political feasibility.[70]

Contribution to Deficit Reduction

The possible contribution of a carbon tax to deficit reduction would depend on the magnitude and scope of the carbon tax, various market factors (discussed above), and assumptions about the size of the deficit. In August 2012, CBO released updated budget projections for fiscal years 2012 to 2022. Under current law, CBO estimated the 10-year budget deficit at $2.3 trillion, or 1.1% of GDP.[71] However, using an alternative fiscal scenario,[72] CBO's projected a larger deficit—$10.0 trillion, or 4.9% of GDP.

Enacting the carbon tax options discussed in the previous section could reduce future budget deficits. As illustrated in **Figure 4**, a $20/mtCO$_2$ price on carbon (increasing by 5.6% annually) would have a considerable impact on budget deficits using CBO's August 2012 baseline projection.

- The 10-year budget deficit could be reduced from $2.3 trillion to $1.1 trillion, or from 1.1% to 0.5% of GDP.

- Overall, a $20/mtCO$_2$ price on carbon would reduce the 10-year budget deficit by more than 50%.

Under CBO's alternative fiscal scenario, the same carbon tax would have a smaller impact on budget deficits.

- The deficit would be reduced from $10.0 trillion to $8.8 trillion, or from 4.9% to 4.4% of GDP.

- Overall, a $20/mtCO$_2$ price on carbon would reduce the 10-year budget deficit by about 12%.

---

[70] See, for example, Dawn Erlandson, "The Btu Tax Experience: What Happened and Why It Happened" *Pace Environmental Law Review* 12, no. 1 (Fall 1994); Lisa Lerer, "Is Cap and Trade Dems' Next 'BTU'?" *Politico*, July 13, 2009; Joseph E. Aldy and Robert N. Stavins, "Using the Market to Address Climate Change: Insights from Theory and Experience," National Bureau of Economic Research Working Paper Series No. 17488 (2011).

[71] The 10-year budget deficit covers fiscal years 2013 through 2022.

[72] This scenario assumes that (1) most expiring tax provisions are extended and the Alternative Minimum Tax (AMT) is adjusted for inflation, (2) Medicare's payment rates for physicians' are held constant at current levels, and (3) that the automatic spending reductions required by the Budget Control Act (BCA) do not occur.

Figure 4. CBO Estimated Revenues from a $20/mtCO$_2$ Carbon Tax Compared to Two CBO Budget Deficit Projections
FY2013-FY2022

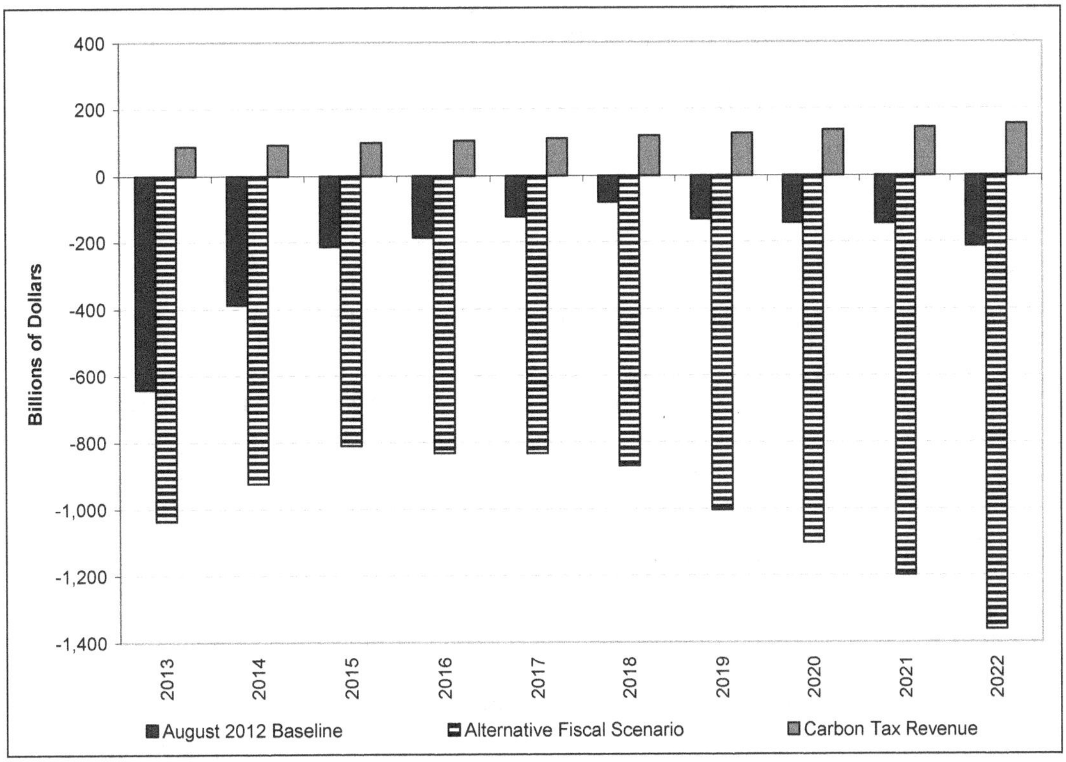

[Bar chart showing Billions of Dollars from 2013 to 2022, comparing August 2012 Baseline, Alternative Fiscal Scenario, and Carbon Tax Revenue]

Source: Prepared by CRS. Carbon tax revenue estimates from CBO, *Reducing the Deficit: Spending and Revenue Options*, Washington, DC, March 2011, pp. 205-206; Budget deficit estimates from CBO, *An Update to the Budget and Economic Outlook: Fiscal Years 2012 to 2022*, August, 2012.

Notes: The 2012 baseline estimates are based on current law. The alternative scenario assumes that (1) most expiring tax provisions are extended and the Alternative Minimum Tax (AMT) is adjusted for inflation, (2) Medicare's payment rates for physicians' are held constant at current levels, and (3) that the automatic spending reductions required by the Budget Control Act (BCA) do not occur. Revenues from the carbon tax are assumed to start in FY2013.

Carbon tax proposals that raise less revenue would contribute less to deficit reduction. The Save Our Climate Act of 2011 (H.R. 3242) states that this legislation would reduce the deficit by $480 billion over the 10-year budget window. Relative to the CBO's alternative fiscal scenario, the $480 billion would reduce the budget deficit by 4.8%, from an estimated $10.0 trillion to roughly $9.5 trillion, or 4.9% to 5.7% of GDP.

The analysis above assumes that 100% of carbon tax revenue would be applied toward deficit reduction. The following section explores possible alternative uses for carbon tax revenues.

Alternative Uses for Carbon Tax Revenues

Carbon tax revenues may be used to achieve a variety of policy goals. However, one revenue use necessarily forgoes the opportunity to apply that level of revenue to support other objectives, like deficit reduction. Therefore, in deciding how to allocate carbon tax revenues, policymakers would encounter trade-offs among objectives. Such trade-offs include

1. minimizing economy-wide costs resulting from a carbon tax;[73]

2. alleviating the costs borne by subgroups in the U.S. population, regions, economic sectors, and generations; and

3. supporting specific policy objectives, such as deficit reduction, climate change mitigation, energy efficiency, technological advances, domestic employment, or energy diversity.

A comprehensive discussion of alternative uses of carbon tax revenues and the involved trade-offs is beyond the scope of this report.[74] Three possible options, which have received some attention in recent years, are discussed below.

Distribute Carbon Tax Revenues to Households

If Congress were to consider a carbon tax system, a key debate would likely involve the degree to which carbon tax revenues would be returned to households to alleviate the expected financial burden imposed by the carbon tax.[75] A 2007 study estimated that households and businesses that are end users would experience the vast majority (89%) of the private costs under a carbon pricing regime (the remaining 13% was attributed to coal, oil, and gas producers and fossil electricity generators).[76] Moreover, businesses—to the extent they were able—would likely pass through to household consumers some of their increased energy/electricity costs in the form of higher prices for their goods and services. Costs that are not passed through to consumers in the form of higher prices are borne by either labor, through reduced wages, or owners of capital, through reduced returns on investment.

Depending on how and to whom carbon tax revenues are distributed, lower-income households could face a disproportionate increase in tax burden. As illustrated in **Table 5**, a carbon tax "in isolation" (i.e., without revenue redistribution of some kind) could have a disproportionately greater impact on lower-income households than higher-income households—a regressive

---

[73] One way to interpret this efficiency objective would be to maximize growth of GDP, though other measures of broader well-being may be an alternative. However, even using a narrow GDP measure would involve decisions about whether economic efficiency pertains to the United States only or international efficiency, or to current taxpayers versus future generations.

[74] For more information, see CRS Report R40242, *Carbon Tax and Greenhouse Gas Control: Options and Considerations for Congress*, by Jonathan L. Ramseur and Larry Parker; and CRS Report R40841, *Assisting Households with the Costs of a Cap-and-Trade Program: Options and Considerations for Congress*, by Jonathan L. Ramseur and Libby Perl.

[75] This issue received considerable attention during the debate over H.R. 2454 ("Waxman-Markey") in the 111th Congress. H.R. 2454, which passed the House on June 26, 2009, would have, among other things, established a price on GHG emissions through a cap-and-trade system.

[76] National Commission on Energy Policy, *Allocating Allowances in a Greenhouse Gas Trading System*, 2007.

outcome.[77] As **Table 5** illustrates, a carbon tax in isolation would reduce after-tax income for taxpayers in the lowest income deciles by 3.4%, while taxpayers in the highest income deciles would see their income fall by 0.8%.[78]

The remaining rows in **Table 5** show how the household impacts would change if carbon tax revenues were rebated to households using different rebate mechanisms.[79]

- An equal lump-sum rebate of carbon tax revenues would be progressive, increasing incomes for those in the lowest income deciles relative to higher-income brackets.[80]

- A payroll tax rebate for workers, in this case, would reduce but not eliminate the regressivity of the carbon tax. Lower-income households without individuals in the workplace would not receive a rebate under this approach.[81]

- Adding a rebate for Social Security recipients to the payroll tax rebate would address the lower-income households with individuals not in the workplace, and further enhance the progressivity of this policy option.[82]

In this scenario, both a lump-sum carbon tax rebate and a carbon tax rebate that includes Social Security recipients increase the after-tax income of lower-income households while decreasing the after-tax income of higher-income households. Using carbon tax revenues to reduce payroll taxes would increase the after-tax income of middle-income households, while lower-income households would see their after-tax income fall.

---

[77] As mentioned above, this is the expected outcome because lower-income households generally spend a higher percentage of their income on energy-related goods and services than do higher-income households.

[78] This study assumed a carbon tax of $15 per ton of CO_2.

[79] For more information on these different mechanisms, see CRS Report R40841, *Assisting Households with the Costs of a Cap-and-Trade Program: Options and Considerations for Congress*, by Jonathan L. Ramseur and Libby Perl.

[80] The per-capita, lump-sum rebate amount assumed in this study was $274.

[81] The credit would cover the first $560 in payroll taxes (or first $3,660 of wages per covered worker, using 2003 data).

[82] Under this option, the maximum credit amount would be $420.

Table 5. Distributional Effects of Carbon Tax with Different Applications of Carbon Tax Revenues

	Percentage Change in After-Tax Household Income by Income Bracket (1= Lowest, 10=Highest)									
Distributional Scenarios	1	2	3	4	5	6	7	8	9	10
Carbon Tax in Isolation (before revenue redistribution)	-3.4	-3.1	-2.4	-2.0	-1.8	-1.5	-1.4	-1.2	-1.1	-0.8
Carbon Tax with a Lump-Sum Distribution to Households	2.1	1.0	0.6	0.4	0.3	0.1	-0.1	-0.1	-0.2	-0.2
Carbon Tax with Payroll Tax Rebate for Workers	-0.7	-1.0	-0.2	0.1	0.1	0.3	0.2	0.2	0.0	0.0
Carbon Tax with Payroll Tax Rebate for Workers and Equivalent Rebate for Social Security Recipients	1.4	1.0	0.6	0.3	0.1	0.1	0.1	-0.1	-0.1	-0.2

Source: Prepared by CRS with data from the following: Gilbert Metcalf, *A Proposal for a U.S. Carbon Tax Swap: An Equitable Tax Reform to Address Global Climate Change* (2007), The Hamilton Project, Brookings Institution.

Note: These results do not account for consumers' behavioral responses to the carbon tax. Metcalf points out that the results provide a "reasonable first approximation" of the different impacts to household incomes (Metcalf (2008)).

Amongst the policies surveyed in **Table 5**, using carbon tax revenues to finance lump-sum rebates to households provides the most benefit to the lowest-income. While enhancing the progressivity of the overall tax system may be attractive from an equity perspective, lump-sum rebates to households offer limited potential for gains in overall economic efficiency. If carbon tax revenues are instead used to offset other distortionary taxes in the economy (i.e., payroll, income), the costs associated with a carbon tax may be reduced or eliminated.

Studies that examine the distribution of a carbon tax rely on a number of modeling assumptions. Metcalf (2007), for example, assumes that the costs of the carbon tax are related to energy expenditure patterns across income groups. An alternative approach is to look at the distribution of the carbon tax, assuming that the carbon tax reduces returns to factors of production: labor, capital, and fossil fuel resources.[83] Under this approach, the regressivity of a carbon tax is reduced. If the burden of the carbon tax falls more heavily on owners of capital, as opposed to labor, the carbon tax affects higher income households that tend to derive more of their income from capital. Further, lower income households that receive a larger share of their income from transfer payments (e.g., social security), would be less affected by a carbon tax. While the "baseline" distribution of a carbon tax (i.e., the distribution of a carbon tax absent revenue recycling) differs under various modeling assumptions, the general conclusions regarding different policy choices for uses of carbon tax revenues often remain the same. Lump-sum

---

[83] Studies that use this approach include Sebastian Rausch, et al., "Distributional Impacts of Carbon Pricing: A General Equilibrium Approach with Micro-Data For Households," *Energy Economics*, vol. 33, no. 1 (March 2011) pp. S20-S33 and Sebastian Rausch, et al., "Distributional Impacts of a U.S. Greenhouse Gas Policy: A General Equilibrium Analysis of Carbon Pricing," in *U.S. Energy Tax Policy*, ed. Gilbert E. Metcalf (Cambridge University Press, 2011), pp. 52-107.

redistribution of carbon tax revenues tends to be more progressive, while policies that reduce payroll taxes tend to be less regressive than those that reduce taxes on income or capital.[84]

Address Economy-Wide Costs

Some are concerned about potential economy-wide costs that a carbon tax would impose. Economy-wide costs, or macroeconomic costs, are often measured in terms of changes in projected gross domestic product (GDP) or another societal-scale metric, such as efficiency cost or welfare changes.

A tax on carbon would likely lead to increased energy costs, which could reduce GDP growth.[85] However, most measures of economic costs imposed by a carbon tax do not consider the climate change benefits or ancillary benefits[86] that a carbon price would provide. The ultimate economic effects would depend on a number of factors, including the magnitude, design, and use of revenues of the carbon tax.

Economic studies indicate that using carbon tax revenues to offset reductions in distortionary taxes—labor, income, and investment—would be the most economically efficient use of the revenues and yield the greatest benefit to the economy overall. Studies also conclude that using tax revenues to lower the federal deficit would yield an economy-wide benefit, because of the reduced need to impose distortionary taxes in the future.[87] But this benefit would be delayed and its realization assumes policymakers would, sometime in the future, address the deficit by raising taxes.

Using carbon tax revenues to offset other distortionary taxes is sometimes described as revenue recycling, a fiscal strategy that may yield a "double-dividend:"[88]

1. reduced GHG emissions, achieved through the new carbon price, and
2. reduced market distortions, achieved through lower taxes on desirable behavior.

---

[84] Sebastian Rausch, et al., "Distributional Impacts of a U.S. Greenhouse Gas Policy: A General Equilibrium Analysis of Carbon Pricing," in *U.S. Energy Tax Policy*, ed. Gilbert E. Metcalf (Cambridge University Press, 2011), pp. 52-107.

[85] Although often used as an economy-wide measurement, GDP is an imperfect measure of the economy or society's well-being. A classic example is that an epidemic may increase measured economic activity because of higher expenditures on health care, while reducing well-being. See also Organisation for Economic Co-operation and Development. How's Life?: Measuring Well-Being. Paris, 2011; Mack Ott, "Limitation of NIA as a Gauge of Welfare" in *The Concise Encyclopedia of Economics: National Income Accounts*, Library of Economics and Liberty, at http://econlib.org/library/Enc/NationalIncomeAccounts.html.

[86] For example, a reduction in GHG emissions from certain sectors may also entail a reduction in hazardous air pollutants, which could provide health-related benefits.

[87] Ian Parry and Robertson C. Williams III, *Moving U.S. Climate Policy Forward: Are Carbon Taxes the Only Good Alternative?* Resources for the Future, 2011; Warwick McKibben et al., *The Potential Role of a Carbon Tax in U.S. Fiscal Reform*, The Brookings Institution, 2012.

[88] For further information, see Ian Parry, "Fiscal Interactions and the Case for Carbon Taxes over Grandfathered Carbon Permits," in *Climate Change Policy* (Dieter Helm, editor), 2005; and Lawrence H. Goulder, "Environmental Taxation and the Double Dividend: A Reader's Guide," *International Tax and Public Finance*, vol. 2, no. 2, 1995, pp. 157-183.

According to a 2011 study,[89] economic literature[90] generally finds that revenue recycling may reduce the economy-wide costs imposed by a carbon tax intended to reduce GHG emissions, but may not eliminate them entirely.[91] However, the same 2011 study and a 2012 study both provide scenarios in which a carbon tax and revenue recycling would produce a net increase in Gross Domestic Product.[92] In other words, these studies found that, in certain situations, that the economic improvements gained by reducing existing distortionary taxes would outweigh the costs imposed by the new carbon tax.[93] In both studies, the potential benefits of reduced GHG emissions were not part of the calculation, largely because these estimates carry considerable uncertainty.

For example, the 2012 study[94] projected a net reduction in GDP and employment—a measure of economy-wide costs—when carbon tax revenues where used to (1) reduce the deficit, (2) provide lump-sum transfers to households, or (3) reduce payroll taxes. However, when carbon tax revenues were used to reduce marginal tax rates on capital income (e.g., the corporate tax), employment and GDP increased relative to the baseline. While using carbon tax revenues to reduce tax rates on capital may enhance economic efficiency, such policies would not offset the increased burden imposed by a carbon tax on low-income households.[95]

Assist Carbon-Intensive, Trade-Exposed Industries

Carbon-intensive, trade-exposed industries would likely face disproportionate impacts within a U.S. carbon tax system. This issue received considerable attention during the debate over H.R. 2454 in 2009 (the 111th Congress) and would likely receive similar attention if Congress were to consider establishing a carbon tax system.

An industry's carbon intensity is a function of both direct CO_2 emissions from its manufacturing process (e.g., CO_2 from cement or steel production) and indirect CO_2 emissions from the inputs to

---

[89] Ian Parry and Robertson C. Williams III, *Moving U.S. Climate Policy Forward: Are Carbon Taxes the Only Good Alternative?* Resources for the Future, 2011.

[90] For example, the following reports found that a price or tax on carbon would have a small, but negative, impact on GDP growth: U.S. Energy Information Administration, *Energy Market and Economic Impacts of H.R. 2454, the American Clean Energy and Security Act of 2009*, Report #: SR-OIAF/2009-05, August 4, 2009, http://www.eia.gov/oiaf/servicerpt/hr2454/background.html and Congressional Budget Office, *The Economic Effects of Legislation to Reduce Greenhouse-Gas Emissions*, Washington, DC, September 2009, http://www.cbo.gov/sites/default/files/cbofiles/ftpdocs/105xx/doc10573/09-17-greenhouse-gas.pdf.

[91] This is referred to as the "tax-interaction effect" in economic literature. See, e.g., Ian Parry, "Fiscal Interactions and the Case for Carbon Taxes over Grandfathered Carbon Permits," in *Climate Change Policy* (Dieter Helm, editor), 2005.

[92] See, e.g., Ian Parry and Robertson C. Williams III, *Moving U.S. Climate Policy Forward: Are Carbon Taxes the Only Good Alternative?* Resources for the Future, 2011; Warwick McKibben et al., *The Potential Role of a Carbon Tax in U.S. Fiscal Reform*, The Brookings Institution, 2012.

[93] Note that this net economy-wide gain does not include benefits achieved by reducing GHG emissions.

[94] This study assumed a tax of $15 per ton of CO_2, with the tax rate rising at 4% above inflation each year through 2050. See Warwick McKibben et al., *The Potential Role of a Carbon Tax in U.S. Fiscal Reform*, The Brookings Institution, 2012

[95] For an analysis of the distribution of federal taxes, including corporate taxes, see Congressional Budget Office, *The Distribution of Household Income and Federal Taxes, 2008 and 2009*, Washington, DC, July 2012, http://www.cbo.gov/sites/default/files/cbofiles/attachments/43373-06-11-HouseholdIncomeandFedTaxes.pdf. The corporate tax is progressive, with 87.4% of the corporate tax burden attributable to the top two income quintiles. Since carbon taxes are regressive, and corporate taxes are progressive, using carbon tax revenues to reduce corporate taxes would tend to reduce the progressivity of the overall tax system.

the manufacturing process (e.g., electricity, natural gas). In general, trade-exposed industries are those that face considerable international competition. A carbon tax would present a particular challenge for these industries. Compared to other domestic industries, they would be less able to pass along the tax in the form of higher prices, because they may lose global market share (and jobs) to competitors in countries lacking comparable carbon policies.[96]

To address these impacts, policymakers could distribute a portion of the carbon tax revenues to these industries. As one point of reference, under H.R. 2454 (111th Congress) such industries would have received approximately 15% of the emission allowance value—analogous to 15% of carbon tax revenue—through 2025, steadily decreasing to zero thereafter. At the time, some questioned whether this allotment was sufficient.[97] Regardless, the data and administrative resources necessary to implement such a program would be substantial.

Alternatively, policymakers could supplement a carbon tax scheme with a border adjustment mechanism that would essentially apply a tariff to carbon-intensive, imported goods. Such a mechanism was included in H.R. 2454 (111th Congress). Under that proposal, EPA would have required importers of energy-intensive products from countries with insufficient carbon policies to submit a prescribed amount of "international reserve allowances," for their products to gain entry into the United States. Implementation of this approach would present substantial administrative challenges, particularly in terms of data from other nations.

In addition, either the revenue distribution or border adjustment approach would likely raise concerns of trade complications. These issues are beyond the scope of this report. For further information, see CRS Report R40914, *Climate Change: EU and Proposed U.S. Approaches to Carbon Leakage and WTO Implications*.

Concluding Observations

Carbon taxes, or fees on emissions of some or all GHG emissions, have been proposed for many years by economists and some Members of Congress. A new carbon price would help reduce GHG emissions contributing to climate change and ocean acidification, and tax revenues could support a range of policy objectives, including deficit reduction.

Carbon tax revenues would depend strongly on the scope and rate of the tax and multiple market factors, which instill uncertainty in revenue projections. A $20/mtCO$_2$ carbon tax on U.S. CO$_2$ emissions would generate approximately $90 billion in its first year. If applied toward deficit reduction, carbon tax revenue (of this magnitude) could have some impact on projected budget deficits, but impacts vary considerably depending on which budgetary baseline is assumed.

Regardless, if policymakers established a carbon tax, they would likely face pressure from multiple stakeholders seeking a portion of the carbon tax revenues. Households would be

---

[96] During debate over H.R. 2454 (in the 111th Congress), the Energy-Intensive Manufacturers' Working Group on Greenhouse Gas Regulation provided detailed testimony on the energy intensity and trade intensity of the U.S. manufacturing sector. Testimony of John McMackin for the Energy Intensive Manufacturers' Working Group on Greenhouse Gas Regulation before the House Committee on Ways and Means (March 24, 2009).

[97] For further details, see CRS Report R40914, *Climate Change: EU and Proposed U.S. Approaches to Carbon Leakage and WTO Implications*.

expected to bear a large portion of burden imposed by a carbon tax. Lower-income households, in particular, would face a disproportionate impact if revenues were not recycled back to them in some fashion. In addition, specific industries may experience disproportionate impacts. Carbon tax revenues that are used to offset the burden imposed on various sectors or specific population groups would not be available to support other objectives, like deficit reduction.

Appendix. Carbon Tax and Carbon Pricing Proposals in the 111th Congress

In the 111th Congress, policymakers introduced at least 9 stand-alone, market-based proposals that sought to reduce GHG emissions.[98] These bills included carbon tax, cap-and-trade, and hybrid approaches. Of the bills that specified a distribution formula for carbon tax revenue or emission allowance value,[99] only three (and one draft bill) would have allotted allowance value or tax revenue that would explicitly support deficit reduction (listed in order of proposed date):

- H.R. 2454 (Waxman-Markey), introduced May 15, 2009: 0.2% of emission allowance value in 2016-2026, zero in subsequent years.

- S. 1733 (Kerry-Boxer), introduced September 30, 2009: 10.3% of emission allowance value in 2016, increasing to 30% in 2030.

- S. 2877 (Cantwell), introduced December 11, 2009: 25% of emission allowance value (subject to the appropriations process) to a fund, which could be used to support a myriad of policy objectives, including deficit reduction.

- Kerry-Lieberman draft legislation, released May 12, 2010: 6.8% of emission allowance value in 2016 and 2030.

Author Contact Information

Jonathan L. Ramseur
Specialist in Environmental Policy
jramseur@crs.loc.gov, 7-7919

Jane A. Leggett
Specialist in Energy and Environmental Policy
jaleggett@crs.loc.gov, 7-9525

Molly F. Sherlock
Specialist in Public Finance
msherlock@crs.loc.gov, 7-7797

---

[98] See CRS Report R40556, *Market-Based Greenhouse Gas Control: Selected Proposals in the 111th Congress*, by Brent D. Yacobucci, and Jonathan L. Ramseur.

[99] Allowance value allocation includes both the use of auction revenues and distribution of allowances to entities (e.g., industry or non-covered parties) at no cost.

www.ingramcontent.com/pod-product-compliance
Lightning Source LLC
Chambersburg PA
CBHW081244180526
45171CB00005B/540